Mercurial

Mercurial

Poems by Allison Joseph

Mayapple Press 2016

Published by   Mayapple Press
                362 Chestnut Hill Road
                Woodstock, NY 12498
                mayapplepress.com

ISBN 978-1-936419-64-7

Library of Congress Control Number 2015920172

ACKNOWLEDGEMENTS

Poems from *Mercurial* previously appeared in the following journals:

Accident, *Pirene's Fountain*; Confederate Season, Sidewalks, Somewhere in the North Bronx, and Late Seventies, *Birmingham Poetry Review*; Her Chair, Pediophobia, Rondeau Redouble for the Women Left Behind, and Ode to Sandals, *ducts.org*; The Pervert's Shoe, *Terminus*; Self-Portrait as Small-Town Bus Depot, *Eccolinguistics*; Period, *Jet Fuel Review*; Ode to the Red Dress, *Dublin Poetry Review*; Skinny, *North Dakota Quarterly*; Different Dozens, *So to Speak*; To Wanderlust, *Cider Press Review*; When You Get Tired of Being Called Ugly, *Crow Hollow 19*.

Cover design by Judith Kerman; cover art used under Creative Commons license from www.torange.us. Photo of author by Rusty Bailey. Book designed and typeset by Amee Schmidt with cover titles in Tangerine, subtitle in Hypatia Sans Pro, poem titles and text in Goudy Old Style.

Contents

Somewhere in the North Bronx, Late Seventies

on the top floor of a sinking two-story,
a girl watches a game with her father,

her sad-eyed, foul-mouthed, quick-
to-anger father. The father loves

the quick bats and ugly spats
of these furious Yankees: hubris

of Jackson bristling with every
swing, every hustle. The girl wants

to go to that stadium, hear the solemn
public address man boom her name,

tell her story. The father eats handfuls
of peanuts, leaves a dirty shell-pile

at the girl's feet, commands her
to pick up his leavings, voice terse

as a strikeout. Her mother—his wife—
works another double shift at Bellevue,

money when money slides out of
the father's hands into one failed

mail-order business after another.
Balls and strikes, hits and losses,

the girl knows them all, sweeps
the pile of leavings into her hands,

father's eyes making sure she's
swept it all up before he rips

open another paunchy bag, crackle
of cellophane crunching between them.

Her Chair

My mother must have been tired
of being mother, wife, some patient's
nurse, tired of a house of dust

and abandoned appliances
drained of their usefulness,
of house keys, doormats,

throbbing of my father's TV
and ringing telephone, his primitive
remote slipping beneath easy

chair cushions. Home from work,
seeing spilled toys, clothes, books,
my dolls with their dead faces,

why was she never tempted
to leave, seek quiet somewhere
besides our crumbling house

with its falling kitchen tiles,
gift-paper skeletons of past
Christmases, fossils of my father's

home improvements, his threadbare
underwear, soiled dress shirts, jeans?
Home from the hospital wards,

long shifts of tending and mending
strangers, didn't she have a right
to refuse us dinner, refuse us

everything? But she came home,
full grocery bags intact despite
her walk from the bus stop,

despite our bathroom clutter
of toothbrushes, washcloths,
kitchen with the broken-clock

oven, living room
with no recliner for her,
no easy chair for her hard work.

Pediophobia

–fear of dolls

Their eyes never close,
these daughters without
mothers—toxic flesh,
curls made of anything

but hair, mouths shaped
into gaping holes
that cry with no voices.
I never wanted that doll

advertised on Saturday
morning TV—"Baby Alive"
whose creepy face
worked an imaginary

bottle, sucking and wetting.
Little bottle, little diaper,
all of it plastic, none
of it real. What was she

preparing us girls for—
with her pink spoon and
food you mixed with water,
only to have her eliminate

it moments later? My
childhood friends coveted
her, tried to shove her
into my arms, but I'd

push her back, not
wanting her ever, no
matter what color
her skin, texture her hair.

Who needs a baby,
I thought, *who will always*
be mute, mimic of life
never living, never breathing?

The Pervert's Shoe

is as glassy and shiny
as retail, crisp as money
new-minted by forgers

wise in the stink
of nightly ink. He has two,
you know, a special

pair silent over parquet
floors and parking lots,
able to burnish

the grime-streaked
corridors of hospitals.
He can find that trap

door you're sure your
landlord nailed shut,
surreptiously unscrewing

your screens off
their hinges, whispering
his way through

your sleep-damp rooms,
until his palm hovers
over your lips, hand

falling ceaselessly
down the second
you awaken to scream.

Different Dozens

—the dozens: African-American comic insult game that begins with
the phrase "your mama"

Your mama's so mystical
she can sit by the right hand of God
and not get dizzy. Your mama's

so spiritual Pope be calling her
for advice, queries left via
official papal voice mail.

Your mama's so remarkable
her prophecies of the future
made Jeane Dixon jealous,

no astrological charts needed
to tell when babies would come,
men leave. Your mama's

so extraordinary she can look
past skin to bone, blood, muscle—
diagnosing bodily ills by passing

her glance over you, seeing
scars on your lungs, toxins
in your cells. Your mama
can walk a tightrope barefoot,

summon new blues from Bessie Smith,
singing what Bessie would sing now,
were she alive. Your mama can
put out fires with a sneeze,

make kitchens clean—never touching
a mop—heal children with the stroke
of a pinky. Your mama smiles,

and my hands feel a swift urge
to shape real birds from clay,
sculpting them so fiercely their wings work.

Accident

Catastrophe looms just a blink away.
It only takes an inch to crash and burn.
Just when our luck runs out, it runs astray.

That bone you thought was strong? It cracked today—
and left you limping, unable now to turn.
Catastrophe blooms just a blink away.

The bullet that mowed down a child at play?
A six-year old confined inside an urn.
Just when our luck runs out, it runs astray.

The freighted train spilled into the bay
to make all drinking sick? We never learn.
Catastrophe balloons. We blink away

despite our rules, despite how loud we pray,
despite all debts, raw bruises that we earn.
Just when our luck runs out, it runs astray.

What can we do, in all our rich dismay?
Keep writing, though it makes us itch and churn.
Catastrophe consumes—one blink away.
And when my luck runs out, I run astray.

Confederate Season

How do you sever heritage from hate,
still fly your flags but not rebuke my skin?
You claim to honor those who helped create
your splendid sense of ancestry, no sin

of slavery implied by ancient flags
unfurling in your yard to honor those
brave men who fell so gallantly, wore rags
on bloody battlefields, who took the blows

of war to save the South, her name. You say
you have no quarrel with me now, that you
will keep the flags on permanent display
despite how frayed they are, no matter who

objects to how they loom above the land,
a country now divided by your stand.

Sidewalks

Why should I be the one who walks afraid,
my shoulders hunched as if I am the one
who's acting criminal, who needs the shade
to hide away the guilt? I haven't done

a thing except remain where I belong—
a woman bound for home or to the store,
whose skirt is short, or straight, or long,
who wears the clothes she likes and nothing more.

Don't tell me I should smile to please your wants;
don't tell me I should stop to talk with you.
Don't tell me what I should or should not flaunt,
what parts of me you're aching to pursue.

I have no need of you, this shouting match.
My body's not a purse for you to snatch.

Pro-Ana

—promotion of the eating disorder anorexia nervosa

She's counting every calorie she eats,
and exercising through all hunger pains,
so weak she's barely steady on her feet,
afraid of any extra ounce she gains.
She strokes her ribs as they cut through her skin,
wants them sharper than knives she aches to scrape
across her bare-boned wrists, the blood within
gone starved of nutrients. Her clothing drapes
the flattened curves she fears will weigh her down.
She worships sunken bellies that she sees
on sites where only thinnest girls abound,
mere thought of fat as hated as disease.
Not knowing how her daughter now behaves,
her mother whispers—*Anna!*—from her grave.

Rondeau Redouble for the Women Left Behind

The women mourn and hoist the coffins high,
limp bodies of their husbands trapped inside.
Shoulders strong, they raise their burdens to the sky,
their sons gone off to war. The coffins ride

upon the strength of women who have cried
for lives they could not save, though they would try
with prayer books and candlelight. Dull-eyed,
the women mourn and hoist the coffins high,

dressed in damp widows' robes, they sanctify
this meager stretch of beach, this grasping tide.
Six women to each box, they dignify
the bodies of their husbands trapped inside,

yes, brothers' bodies too—no males to guide
the village out of misery, no men to mollify
the constant threat of death, of genocide.
Shoulders strong, they raise their burdens to the sky,

their voices snagged in hymn, they glorify
the Savior leading them to riverside
where they will let these burdens go. Goodbye
to sons gone off to war. The coffins ride

until they sink into the splash, collide
and bang against the riverbank, deny
an easy grief. Such pain too raw to just subside,
their voices surge and amplify,
the women mourn.

Fault

I'm a fan of the lost cause and the mouthy
female, the half-filled auditorium
and the half-written song, botched

surgeries and bad toupees. See my
stitching crookedly sprawling
across this fabric, these factory

seconds, this sweat-stained white
blouse from my junior-high chorus
class uniform, gym shorts shrunken

doll-size by the Kenmore's machinations?
The only ways in which I'm worthy
are the ways in which I'm unworthy:

sixth-place science fair ribbons,
bundt cake baked in the square
pan, grand sweep of my hand

that sends my water glass crashing
to the floor of a restaurant I dared
dine in, given the holes in my stockings

and eyesight, worn-down
pumps I've crammed my toes into
so when the waiter slides me

my check, holds open the door,
I stumble to stand, spill cash on
the table, my credit no good here.

To Wanderlust

You touch me and I go all directions at once—
wayward, starstruck by street signs
and alleyways, hopped up on a muddy trail's
unfamiliar suck, jazzed by brick roads
and cul-de-sacs, detours and avenues.
My enemy is the stop sign, red lollipops
impeding progress when I want to run
past their warning onto the next block,
next intersection, next city and town—
all of them discoveries I want to cruise,
rolling the names of dive bars on my tongue,
wiping my dusty soles on the welcome mat
of any family-run restaurant where waitresses
sigh an unfettered sigh and slip me
the biggest piece of pie or cake or chicken.
They too want to be touched by you,
to drop their aprons behind the counter,
saying sayonara to the bus boys, fry cooks.
You make us want to whistle goodbye
to the cash's register's clang, the door
bell's ring, the desk's stolid chair.
You dance us to the end of one-lane highways,
places the GPS shuts off, dots on the map
so miniscule we squint to see them—
tiny etchings on a grid, blue lines like veins.

Curse Poem to the Weather Channel

How dare you name a common winter
storm, interrupt my dozing with continual
proclamations of meteorological doom,

haunting my nights with forecasts
that make me clench and shudder
under my stockade of blankets?

Local on the 8's aside, what do you
give that doesn't turn me
into a chattering bucket of ice water,

frozen yet shivering, unable to rise
from bed to coffeepot? All you brew
is trouble—wrecked seas, nauseous

rocking, waves I tumble in, everyday
a never-ending drowning. If I ever
see one of your reporters nattering

for the camera on my street,
yelling all that turbulence to come,
I'm leaving town, belongings packed

in a bundle on a stick, last food
stuffed in my thirsty pockets.
Hell if I'm going to lie around

waiting for your heated prophecies
to come true. I don't need a tornado
to hit me in the head to learn

whether or not I'm one of the lucky
few, the chosen people. I'm escaping
now, my head full of barometric

pressure, my temperature,
on this record-breaking day,
too faint for Fahrenheit or Celsius.

Metabolism

You were so special,
and I took you for granted,
thinking we'd always be
together, you fierce enough

to burn off whatever junk
I infested myself with,
stoked simply by my
shuddering, boy-crazy heart.

I thought you'd never
get old, never slow,
never leave me crying
in a fitting room,

stalled over pants
not zipping up over thighs
grown wide with age,
the constant splay

of sitting. Now, I
goose you with caffeine,
give side-eye to sleight-
of-hand fat burning

pills in magazine ads,
ridiculous claims
to slim me quick
as ubiquitous as

the latest celebrity
scandals, all greasy
pics and twitter splatter.
Now, you want to live

life real lazy, all
languid and dreamy,
middle-age bulge
solid as milkfat,

as curds, not whey.
Why fight this inevitable
deceleration, I think,
why trot in these

endless circles,
legs kicking behind me
in a attempt to keep
you firing, me alive?

You school me daily,
warn me weekly,
say my name
and scare me silly—

all in the name of burning
all that I must burn,
the fires that keep me
mouthing the cold moist air.

Self-Portrait as Small-Town Bus Depot

My waiting room reeks of escape—
all the parcels and suitcases stacked
and shoved into the bellies

of lumbering motorcoaches,
stale bags of chips and pretzels
in my last-quarter-to-my-name

vending machine. If you call me
desperate, I won't disagree—years
of slashes on my vinyl seats,

spilled sodas on my linoleum,
scrawled numbers on my bathroom
walls long since disconnected,

those good times had by souls
long gone. I am only open
one hour each day, locked up

between arrivals and departures
as if I'm precious, as if glass
isn't shattered on my front steps

by the last indigent in town
who hasn't moved to higher
ground. I am sinking, bit by

bit, ceiling peeling like a
shredded skin, paint on my walls
laden with sticky prints, scuff

marks. Dingy, dirty, damaged,
I am your one way out of
this place, so you better listen

when your destination is called—
that last bus out of town
waiting for you to climb on,

wipe someone else's sweat
off the seat, and fall into the haze
of the one road out of here.

Columbia Record and Tape

All that music for a penny made me greedy,
made me believe Terre Haute, Indiana must
be an entertainment mecca, music flowing
everywhere—every street corner and alley,

hot tub and day care center, this Club
a lot more hip than the Book-of-the-Month Club,
more fun than the fake leather tomes
and busted collector plates my father bought

from Franklin Mint. Never thought to call up
the Club, demand they take back what
I wasn't swift enough to reject, though now
a friend tells me he worked there during

college, fielded call after call from unhappy
music lovers, angry people who got Mandrill
when they wanted Mozart, REO when
they wanted Rachmaninoff. The Club

made you declare your musical allegiance,
though you could order from any category,
tried to make you define what you wanted
while tempting you with everything you

ever might have wanted—bargain-bin
dwellers *going going gone,* music-by-mail-
order somehow sweeter when I'd spend
hours on my bed, twirling the pages

of their slick catalog, peering at
shrunken photos of singers in fetching
'80s finery, pen circling and circling,
taking a chance on some group I'd never

heard before, obsessions begun in the heat
of my slovenly teenage bedroom,
all the hooks I ever wanted to hold
coming straight out of Terre Haute.

Aubade in Which I Always Return

While you sleep, mask tethering you
to breath, machine pushing dreams into you,
past your body's reluctance to sink
into sacred REM, I lace up sneakers,
slip out our cluttered house's side door,

body and limbs waking into ache
as I start that morning's run, legs finding
their rhythm over sidewalk cracks and gashes
in blacktop, hips my true center of motion,
propulsion echoing with each footfall.

I've pledged these hips to you, and you
have loved them no matter their size,
amplification and diminution of flesh,
stretch marks lightly scoring my skin.
How brave it is to love a real woman,

cherish the stink of her sweat and hair,
unpainted face and chafed skin, rigor
of sunburn and windburn. And you have
loved me with constant courage, diligent heart,
encouraging miles that start in morning's

semi-dark, elusive hour of promise or failure,
growing light making plain stealthy shapes
of squirrels or birds, trees turning back
into trees from skeletal ghosts, shifting
in irrepressible gusts. I let the miles collect,

trust in this body you have given
your trust, know you wait for me in your
assisted sleep, know when I stumble
out my last steps, turn the key in our house's
testy lock, you will ditch the mask,

rise to breathe on your own,
to hold these hips, this sore triumph
I only enact knowing I'll be back
for you to ask how I ran:
how long, how far, how fast.

Ode to Sandals

How I've missed your open
comfort, your leather against bare skin,
summer sun on straps, holding

my feet in with the ease
only you provide. All this brutish winter,
with its jagged winds and icy

spiteful sleet, I dreamed of you,
of slipping my feet into you and striding
off into a new adventure,

getting lost in damp grass newly
wet from a neighbor's trippy sprinkler.
You hate formalities, and I

love your aimless sexy ways,
keeping me vulnerable
but shod, strapped around my ankles

like a gladiator's, jubilant
as I skip over stones and muddy puddles,
sidewalks and streams, toes

bold to get wet, all the world
lush with drinking spring, humid breath
of summer lurking beneath.

You make me strut, greatest
dancer in the kingdom. I slip you on and off
like a changeling, wear you barelegged

with swirling skirts. You care
not for how much I weigh, if my back aches.
Contained by you, my feet swell with joy.

Ode to the Red Dress

Forget little black anything.
A woman in a black dress
is mourning, no matter where
she goes in sky-high heels
or sweet sashay.

A woman in a red dress
is lighting her skin from
within, sending radiance,
diligence—fingertips
sleek over a slide of curves.

The red dress dances
while the black dress sulks,
the red dress pops its buttons
while the black dress denies
you its zipper, guarding

everything with a smirk,
finite dismissal of a wave.
Beast of a color, transfer
of heat and power, light
blush to quick flame,

the red dress giggles,
unafraid of wine, sweat,
scandals. Take that red dress
out of your closet
and put it on your body

where it belongs,
so your blood can divulge
its secrets. A woman
in a red dress has
no need of secrets,

of shame, of the sour
hurt that could mark

her face like a bruise,
a scar. A woman
in a red dress

is a vice, a crevice,
space you beg to occupy,
empty box now full,
thermometer's mercury
now burst from slender glass.

Period

Little black globe of authority,
finality, you are the world's
freckle, dot that hard-smacks me
at the end of sentences I'm not
even sure I should have written.
Bullet for the broken-hearted,
fleck of fear, speck that burns
when I try to flick it off the page,
stuck solemn as a street sign,
full stop my fingers obey, eyes
honor. Such power in something
so small, seemingly insignificant
but never scarce. How is it
you get to dictate all our
beginnings, endings, so smug
in potent squalor, ubiquitous
beyond all reason. If I leave
you out, skip you, ignore you,
you only call attention through
your absence, haunting as you
disappear. You speak
the unspeakable braille,
send messages that pierce
and shatter, little dagger,
eyedropper, final stitch
in the fabric of the word.

Skinny

As a child, I hated that word—
hurled at me like a curse,
lips sucked in disgust over
my bony knees, lattice of
rib cage and clavicle, lack
of curves marking me as
suspect, stark mutant not fit
for adolescence. So when
you call me skinny now,
your compliments on lost
pounds and dropped sizes
send me someplace far darker
than you know: terrorscape
of somatic fears and teenage
taunts, maze of insecurities
more slippery than a winter
sidewalk. I did not lose
to enter the shrine of skinny,
join the cult of before-and-
after photos, diet confessionals,
to slip into some long-coveted
outfit: some star-spangled
bikini or Victoria's Secret
swath of pink. I lost so I
could live to write more,
family spectre of diabetes
lifted, high blood pressure
beaten back by well-worn
sneakers. Poetry tastes better
than skinny feels, and if
this loss gifts me with more
days, I will breathe, write,
run and live, skinny girl
I was loved, fat woman
I was loved, all those selves
coming to this page, singing.

When You Get Tired of Being Called Ugly

"I think that beauty is subjective. I've heard that statement my entire life, being a dark-skinned black woman... 'classically not beautiful' is a fancy term for saying ugly... It worked when I was younger. It no longer works for me now."
—Viola Davis, actress

When you get tired of being called ugly,
you lift your head out of your shoulders,
elevate your chin to let all that regal richness
pour forward from you, echoes of your skin
saturating the air around you. You are
no one's lesser, smile playing around
your lips no tease, no smirk, but radiance,
righteous radiance. You are a straight spine
in the sun, glissando arch of a bare foot,
legacy of hurt on limbs shed like so many
calluses, layers of rejection and ache
sloughed off like so many unraveled
nooses. When you get tired, completely
and unequivocally tired, your voice
becomes ravishment, enchantment,
glorious as the very last slow dance
on the very last night of forever,
because your eternity rises up and out
into cities, turning statutes into statues,
law into light. When you, undeniably
and unforgettably you, rise in the morning,
you greet your own face with the knowledge
no stranger can stop the lucent thrill
behind your eyelids, the dazzling
obsidian joy you've found beneath the tips
of your own palms, your own fingers.

Ballade for Motherless Daughters

–for Brett

We wake at night, scan picture frames
to keep her face in memory,
that countenance always the same
in photos of shared history,
a past from which our futures flee,
a future that's exempt from her.
Time rushes us, until we'll be
much older than our mothers ever were.

Her face, her smile—both make their claim.
See how our features still agree?
Some days, that grief cannot be tamed,
it rides your tongue, won't shake you free,
despite long baths, some good chablis.
Her loss will always reoccur,
despite new cars, advanced degrees.
Much older than our mothers ever were,

we'll tell our daughters how they got their names,
their grandmothers alive in legacy.
Our sons will know just what she overcame.
To fill blank space on a family tree,
we'll speak her name aloud, and reverently
remember words she said, songs she preferred.
We'll touch those photographs, though we'll soon be
much older than our mothers ever were.

We speak from knowing grief's agility;
with elegies, we've grown to be secure.
Each day's a test of our abilities,
much older than our mothers ever were.

Aubade with New Poem

She's small, quiet on my lips
and fingertips, no meaty epic.
Yet she wants to rise and sing

before I want to rise and walk,
phrases flaring beneath
my half-mast eyelids. Trickle

that yearns to spill onto paper,
I bid her hush, not now,
let me brush the webs of sleep

from my eyes before you
throttle me with your one
insistent whisper, your

siren slither. You don't care
that I'm unwashed, uncaffeinated—
you are queen of urgent

utterance, mistress of crafty
syllables and stutter-breath
breaks, bully before breakfast.

If I rise and play with you,
what will you yield,
how will you sound—

you mad morning dash,
you sudden leap of lines?
You won't let me lie

in this ragtag pile of pillows
and blankets until I tuck
into you, begin to love

you—little racecar, little
hovercraft, small vibrant thing
I can't bear to crush.

About the Author

Allison Joseph lives, writes, and teaches in Carbondale, Illinois, where she is part of the creative writing faculty at Southern Illinois University. She serves as editor and poetry editor of *Crab Orchard Review*, moderator of the Creative Writers Opportunities List, and director of the Young Writers Workshop, a summer writers workshop for teen writers.

Her books and chapbooks include *What Keeps Us Here* (Ampersand Press), *Soul Train* (Carnegie Mellon University Press), *In Every Seam* (University of Pittsburgh), *Wordly Pleasures* (Word Tech), *Imitation of Life* (Carnegie Mellon UP), *Voice: Poems* (Mayapple Press), *My Father's Kites* (Steel Toe Books), *Trace Particles* (Backbone Press), *Little Epiphanies* (Imaginary Friend Press), *Multitudes* (Word Tech Communications), *The Purpose of Hands* (Glass Lyre Press), and *Mortal Rewards* (White Violet Press).

She is the literary partner and wife of Jon Tribble.

Other Recent Titles from Mayapple Press:

Jean Nordhaus, *Memos from the Broken World*, 2016
 Paper, 80pp, $15.95 plus s&h
 ISBN 978-936419-56-2
Doris Ferleger, *Leavened*, 2015
 Paper, 64pp, $15.95 plus s&h
 ISBN 978-936419-47-0
Helen Ruggieri, *The Kingdom Where No One Keeps Time*, 2015
 Paper, 80pp, $15.95 plus s&h
 ISBN 978-936419-55-5
Jan Bottiglieri, *Alloy*, 2015
 Paper, 82pp, $15.95 plus s&h
 ISBN 978-936419-52-4
Kita Shantiris, *What Snakes Want*, 2015
 Paper, 74pp, $15.95 plus s&h
 ISBN 978-936419-51-7
Devon Moore, *Apology from a Girl Who Is Told She Is Going to Hell*, 2015
 Paper, 84pp, $15.95 plus s&h
 ISBN 978-1-936419-54-8
Sara Kay Rupnik, *Women Longing to Fly*, 2015
 Paper, 102pp, $15.95 plus s&h
 ISBN 978-1-936419-50-0
Jeannine Hall Gailey, *The Robot Scientist's Daughter*, 2015
 Paper, 84pp, $15.95 plus s&h
 ISBN 978-936419-42-5
Jessica Goodfellow, *Mendeleev's Mandala*, 2015
 Paper, 106pp, $15.95 plus s&h
 ISBN 978-936419-49-4
Sarah Carson, *Buick City*, 2015
 Paper, 68pp, $14.95 plus s&h
 ISBN 978-936419-48-7
Carlo Matos, *The Secret Correspondence of Loon and Fiasco*, 2014
 Paper, 110pp, $16.95 plus s&h
 ISBN 978-1-936419-46-3
Chris Green, *Resumé*, 2014
 Paper, 72pp, $15.95 plus s&h
 ISBN 978-1-936419-44-9

For a complete catalog of Mayapple Press publications, please visit our website at *www.mayapplepress.com*. Books can be ordered direct from our website with secure on-line payment using PayPal, or by mail (check or money order). Or order through your local bookseller.